C000199946

EASTERN COACH WORKS

Peter Horrex

AMBERLEY

First published 2017

Amberley Publishing
The Hill, Stroud
Gloucestershire, GL5 4EP

www.amberley-books.com

Copyright © Peter Horrex, 2017

The right of Peter Horrex to be identified as
the Author of this work has been asserted in
accordance with the Copyrights, Designs and
Patents Act 1988.

ISBN 978 1 4456 6952 6 (print)
ISBN 978 1 4456 6953 3 (ebook)

British Library Cataloguing in Publication Data.
A catalogue record for this book is available from
the British Library.

Origination by Amberley Publishing.
Printed in the UK.

Introduction

Eastern Coach Works of Lowestoft in Suffolk is probably best known for building bus bodies fitted on to a chassis built by Bristol Commercial Vehicles, though coach and lorry bodywork was also produced. Opened in 1921 while under the ownership of United Automobile Services, the East Anglian part of United was given over to a newly formed company named Eastern Counties in 1931, and subsequently the body-building plant was separated from Eastern Counties in 1936 to become known as Eastern Coach Works Limited, growing to be one of Lowestoft's largest employers, with over 1,000 employees at its peak.

Nationalised in 1947, the plant concentrated mainly on building bus bodies for state-owned companies, until 1965 when a 25 per cent share was sold to Leyland Motors that allowed ECW to sell their products to the private sector. With the formation of the National Bus Company in 1969, ECW became jointly owned with British Leyland. In 1982 NBC sold its share to British Leyland, who in turn closed the business in 1987.

Eastern Coach Works are probably best remembered in their heyday for their bodies that were carried by Bristol K, Lodekka, MW, RE, LH and VR buses.

My interest in buses began as a teenager back in 1976, growing up just outside Ipswich in Suffolk, with Eastern Counties as my local operator. By now we were coming in to the heyday of the National Bus Company era, and I enjoyed my weekly day out every Saturday, usually around East Suffolk, forming my love for anything with the Bristol/ECW combination. Having been an enthusiast for over forty years, I have also been a bus driver now for over thirty, mainly in London, but I have worked for Eastern Counties in my home town as well, just catching the last years of Bristol VR operation there.

Invaluable in researching the text for this book have been the following websites:

Bristol Commercial Vehicles Enthusiasts by Rob Sly: http://bcv.robsly.com/
Bus lists on the web: http://www.buslistsontheweb.co.uk/
Bristol Vehicles: http://www.bristolsu.co.uk/

Peter Horrex
Enfield, Middlesex
June 2017

Eastern Counties FLF441 (GPW 441D), a 1966 FLF6G, powers its way along Bell Lane in Kesgrave, Suffolk, in 1980, working service 244 to Melton. Nearing the end of crew operation at Ipswich, this route, along with the Felixstowe services, was the last remaining stronghold here for the Lodekka. Crew operation with Eastern Counties at Ipswich ended on 3 January 1981.

Eastern Counties Lodekka FLF440 (GPW 440D) and Bristol RE RLE869 (WPW 869H) stand in the Old Cattle Market bus station in Ipswich in 1979.

Bristol LH HJT 45N was new to Hants & Dorset in March 1975 as an LH6L with ECW B43F bodywork. She is seen here in Exeter in 1997 working for Stagecoach as a driver training vehicle.

South Shields Busways 1813 (OWC 722M) is a Bristol RELL6L that was new to Colchester Borough Transport in December 1973, passing to Busways in September 1988. She is seen here passing through South Shields in 1991. Happily, this RE survives in preservation today.

Eastern Counties LFS109 (ENG 109C) is a Bristol Lodekka FS5G that was new in June 1965, and is seen here in Ipswich in 1979. By this time just eight Lodekkas were in use at Ipswich – four of the FS variety, and four of the longer FLF type. LFS109 was withdrawn and sold in July 1980, passing through Ben Jordan of Coltishall to Viv Carter, Colchester, in January 1981.

A few Lodekkas over the years had extended lives, after being converted into tow trucks. Eastern Counties X55 (47 CNG), new in May 1963, rescues VR405 (KPW 405L) in Woodbridge Road, Ipswich, in 1981. She had been converted to a towing vehicle in February 1975 and continued as such until withdrawal in 1989.

Bristol VR EWN 993W was new to South Wales as 993 in 1980. She is seen here in Neath in 1992, heading for Swansea.

This Bee Line Bristol VR WJM 819T, seen here in Slough on 22 May 1993, is a VRT/SL3/6LXB with ECW H43/31F bodywork. She was new to Alder Valley as fleet number 959 in December 1978.

Bristol RE AFM 113G was new to Crosville Motor Services in April 1969 as fleet number SRG113. Remaining part of the Crosville Wales fleet after deregulation in 1986, she was finally withdrawn in December 1990, being one of the two final REs in this fleet, passing to Northern Bus of Anston where she remained for eight years before passing into preservation in 1998. She is seen here in Dinnington in 1992.

Eastern Counties LH919 (TCL 139R) was new in May 1977, and was a regular vehicle at the East Bergholt out-station. Eastern Counties withdrew some of their LHs after a relatively short lifespan, and 919 was withdrawn in March 1984, less than seven years old. She is seen here in Ipswich in 1980 alongside LH523 (CNG 523K).

A crisp winter's day on 12 December 1981, and Ipswich-based Bristol RE RL667 (PPW 667F) collects passengers in Claydon, bound for her home town on route 218. RL667 is an RELL6G with Eastern Coach Works B53F bodywork and was new in May 1968. She was withdrawn in July 1984 and scrapped.

Seen in Stockton-on-Tees in 1991 is ex-London Transport Bristol LH KJD 421P, working for Robson. This LH6L was new to London Transport in June 1976, though it was acquired by Robson from Cheery Tree coaches in June 1989, and was subsequently sold on in April 1994 to Express Motors of Kirkby-in-Ashfield.

Carters Coach Services SVW 274K is a 1972 Bristol RELL6G that was new to Eastern National. She passed to the Essex County Council education department in 1985, remaining here until withdrawal in 1992. Acquired by Carters in 1994, she worked in service for a number of years before being preserved. In 2007 she is seen at Holbrook in Suffolk on a special RE day that saw her in use on a variety of Carters routes. In 2013 she passed to Luke Deal of Colchester for further preservation.

Eastern Counties service 221 linked Mistley with Ipswich, though there were some short workings to and from Cattawade, of which this was one. A Saturday morning in 1980 and VR377 (UAH 377G) collects passengers in Stutton bound for Ipswich, despite displaying that commonly used destination of 'SERVICE' that was favoured by Eastern Counties.

Eastern Counties' 204 service was a four-hour round trip between Ipswich and Bury St Edmunds, and was jointly worked from both depots. A busy and popular route, Ipswich always tended to allocate its newest Bristol VR to the route, and as such VR243 (JAH 243V) was known by staff here as the 'Bury Bus'. New in November 1979, she is seen here a couple of months later in January 1980 at Woolpit, Bury St Edmunds bound.

Deep in the Suffolk countryside in the picturesque village of Laxfield, Eastern Counties VR396 (ENG 396K) is about to turn around during her journey from Ipswich to Stradbroke in 1980. VR396, along with sister VR398, were unusual at Ipswich in having the door operation controlled using the gear select lever. As the cash tray was fitted underneath the motorised unit that powered the Setright ticket machine, opening the flap on the cash tray would knock the selector into the neutral position, thus closing the doors on boarding passengers!

Preserved Eastern National Bristol Lodekka AVX 975G is seen in Walthamstow on 28 April 2013, on the occasion of one of the route 251 running days, remembering the old Eastern National service between Southend and Wood Green. This FLF6G was new in August 1968.

Bristol RELL6G CVW 858G was new to Eastern National in February 1969. Passing to the dealer Ensign in 1983, she came to Rallybeam of Debach in Suffolk in 1984, trading as Felixstowe Omnibus. She is seen here in 1986 in between journeys at Woodbridge, displaying route 49 on what would have been a service serving the local St Audreys Hospital.

On 12 December 1981, Eastern Counties PPW 667F failed at Colchester with a puncture, and Eastern National duly loaned one of their own Bristol REs, CR1521 (HTW 179H), which is seen here having arrived at Ipswich. New in 1970, this RE survived just thirteen years before being scrapped in 1983.

A pair of Eastern Counties Bristol VRs pass each other at Wickham Market in 1982. VR292 (VEX 292X) was in the care of the small depot at Saxmundham, while VR204 (XNG 204S) was working the first Saturday journey of the day from Stradbroke to Ipswich by the Woodbridge outstation. VR204 was one of two buses at Ipswich to receive this all-over advertising for Suffolk's two local radio stations.

In 1985 Eastern Counties acquired a batch of second-hand Bristol VRs from Ribble. OCK 990K, which was new in 1972 as Ribble 1990 became VR402 in her new owner's fleet, and was surprisingly still in NBC livery when photographed at Felixstowe in 1990.

The Old Cattle Market bus station in Ipswich is the location for this snowy scene on 12 December 1981 as a variety of Eastern Counties buses stand in the cold awaiting their next spell of duty. Identifiable in the photo are Bristol RE RL680 (RAH 680F), VR241 (JAH 241V) and nearest the camera VR191 (TEX 401R).

Cambus 751 was originally Eastern Counties VR298 (VEX 298X), delivered new in September 1981 and passing to Cambus on the formation of that company in September 1984. She is seen here in Cambridge in 1996.

Hants & Dorset Bristol LH 3537 (ORU 537M) was one of the buses with the cut-down front for use on the Sandbanks Ferry; she is seen leaving the ferry in 1981. New in May 1974, she was withdrawn in 1983, but held as engineering stock until 1985. She was subsequently exported to an unknown owner in St Johns, Antigua.

Northern Bus OHU 36M is a Bristol RELL that was new to the Bristol Omnibus Company in October 1973. She was sold to Cumberland in 1986 before passing to Citybus a year later. She came to Northern Bus of North Anston in 1991, and is seen here in Sheffield on 12 September 1992.

Eastern Counties VR198 (TEX 408R) at Tattingstone in 1986. She was new in May 1977 and by the time this photo was taken she was allocated to the out-station at Sudbury, having gained the name *Thomas Gainsborough*, as displayed above the front grill.

A Saturday Hadleigh out-station duty on a damp day in 1980, as Eastern Counties VR368 (TNG 368G) collects passengers in Ipswich bound for Sudbury on route 205. New in May 1969, though the exact date of her withdrawal is not known, she survived in the fleet at least until 1986. She was subsequently scrapped.

Eastern Counties Bristol MW5G 3014 AH was new in March 1959 as LL452. She was converted for driver-only operation the following year, and the fleet number was also changed to LM452. She was again renumbered in 1965 to LM952. Withdrawn in 1974, she was owned by John Brignell & Co. (builders) of Cambridge in 1975, before passing into preservation in 1978. This view is in Norwich in 2006 as part of the Eastern Counties 75th anniversary celebrations.

A rear view here showing the neat rear-end styling of Badgerline Bristol VR EWS 753W at Chippenham on 18 May 1992. Delivered new to the Bristol Omnibus Company in August 1981, she became part of the Badgerline fleet in 1986 before entering the preservation scene in 2006. She still survives in preservation today.

A flat-screened Bristol RE that still survives today in preservation is TRY 118H. New to Leicester Corporation at the end of 1969, she was one of a batch that were acquired by the Borough of Ipswich in 1980. In this 1985 view she is seen having just arrived at the Tower Ramparts bus station in Ipswich.

Eastern Coach Works-bodied Leyland Olympian C38 CHM was new to London Buses in March 1986 as L38. By 2002, when this photo was taken, she had found her way to Arriva in Hertfordshire, though still working in to the outskirts of London on route 310, which operated in those days from Hertford to Enfield Town. In full Arriva livery she stands in the small bus station at Little Park Gardens in Enfield.

The small village of Levington, on the outskirts of Ipswich in Suffolk, is probably most famous for Fisons Levington Compost, which was developed here. On this occasion, however, we see the attractive lines of Eastern Counties flat-screened VR390 (BNG 452J) at Levington village hall on 10 April 1982, having arrived from Ipswich on the short 250 service. New in June 1971, she was to be withdrawn and scrapped by Eastern Counties without seeing further use elsewhere, though the exact date of scrapping is unknown.

One of my favourite photos that compares nicely the two common fronts on the Bristol RE series, with Eastern Counties flat-screened RL680 (RAH 680F) nearest the camera and later-styled curve-screened RL507 (CNG 507K), both standing in Ipswich in 1980 flanked by Bristol VR258 (RAH 258W).

Owned by David Edwards, this splendidly preserved Eastern National Bristol RE FWC 439H is seen here on 28 April 2013 in Romford. New in December 1969, she passed from Eastern National to Ensign (dealer) in 1983, then finding use with Kent County Council in Margate as a caravan. Further use in the early nineties in Peterborough also as a caravan, she entered the preservation scene in 1996, before passing on to David in 2001.

A further view of David Edwards' preserved Eastern National Bristol RE FWC 439H, this time showing the driver's cab area.

Bristol VR CBV 9S was new in August 1977 to Ribble Motor Services, being withdrawn in 1993 and passing to Milton Keynes City bus. In January 1997, while working for MK Metro, she was de-roofed under a low bridge, and subsequently she passed to Guide Friday of Stratford-upon-Avon, where she was converted to B31F. In 2001 she passed to Carters of Ipswich, and she is seen here at Carters' premises in Capel St Mary in 2001, still wearing Guide Friday livery. By 2010 she had been broken up onsite, providing spares for the restoration of VR VEX 294X.

Eastern Counties LH930 (WEX 930S) received dual-purpose livery and coach seats during the mid-1980s. In this 1986 view she is in the care of the Woodbridge outstation, collecting passengers at Pulham St Mary, working route 859 to Harleston, where the driver had an approximate layover of a couple of hours before working the return journey back to Pulham Market and Stradbroke. New in April 1978, she passed to Tyne and Wear Omnibus in 1989, then on to Bedlington and District of Ashington, before being scrapped in 1993.

Elderly Bristol VRs on the Ipswich to Colchester service were somewhat a rarity from the late seventies onwards, as a union agreement at Ipswich dictated that the newest VRs should be used on routes with dual carriageway working. However, Eastern Counties VR368 (TNG 368G) made it to Colchester in 1981, where she is seen collecting passengers for the return journey to Ipswich.

In Norwich in September 2006, on the occasion of Eastern Counties' 75th anniversary celebrations, is preserved Bristol RE KVF 658E, which was new in 1967.

And again, another view of KVF 658E in Norwich, this time showing the neat rear-end styling of the ECW body. She is owned by the Eastern Transport Collection and is well-known on the rally circuit.

United Automobile Services 1706 (LPT 706T) was a Bristol LH that was new in 1979. Seen here departing Ripon in 1991 for York wearing Ripon Citybus livery, she passed to Tees and District in 1994 before moving on two years later to Cygnet of Darton. Acquired by Rapson of Brora in 1997, she was subsequently scrapped in 2006.

Shanklin on the Isle of Wight is the location for this 1993 view of a pair of Southern Vectis Bristol VRs. ODL 666R, to the left of the photo, was new in 1977 and entered the preservation scene in 2005 before suffering terminal engine failure in 2012, which resulted in her being scrapped. UDL 669S was new in 1978, entered the preservation scene in 1997, and still survives today.

Bristol RE SVF 896G was new to Eastern Counties in February 1969 and remained with this operator until September 1981, where she passed via Jordan (dealer) of Coltishall to Carters of Colchester. In this 1991 view she is seen in Colchester, collecting passengers for service 247 to Dedham.

PWY 39W is a Bristol VR that was new in December 1980 to the West Yorkshire Road Car Company. After a spell with York City and District she began her journey south in April 1990 when she moved to Peterborough-based Viscount Bus & Coach, remaining there until 1996. She then worked for Hedingham and District until 2010, when she passed via Ensign (dealer) to Travel with Hunny of Romford. Waltham Cross bus station is the location for this 2010 view, as she works TWH service 555, which operated to and from Harlow.

Eastern Counties RLE746 (GCL 348N) was part of a batch of eight dual-purpose Bristol RELHs delivered in 1974, at a time when deliveries of the RE to the National Bus Company was coming to an end, with the Leyland National being the preferred choice of single-deck bus. This entire batch passed to Cambus ten years later when Eastern Counties was split pending deregulation. In this 1981 view RLE746 poses for the camera at Felixstowe Dock on the 253 variant of the Ipswich to Felixstowe service.

Ipswich in 1980 is the location for this view showing two differing body styles carried by the Bristol LH. On the left is LH909 (YAH 909J), a flat-screened Bristol LH6P that was new in October 1970, and scrapped ten years later in 1981. On the right is a later curved-screened example, LH919 (TCL 139R), new in 1977 and withdrawn when just a few years old in 1984. She was sold on to Peter England Shirts, Magherafelt, to be subsequently scrapped the following year.

Having arrived from Ipswich on the short 220 service, Eastern Counties RL501 (APW 501J) has just turned around at Harkstead before working the return journey back in to town in 1980; limited services to Harkstead were eventually incorporated as through journeys to Shotley via Erwarton. New in February 1971, RL501 was scrapped in March 1986.

Eastern National 4016 (C416 HJN) is an ECW-bodied Leyland Olympian that was new in 1986. She is seen here ten years later passing through Colchester.

27 August 2011 was the occasion of one of the Ensign Bus running days, centred on the Lakside shopping centre. Splendidly restored Royal Blue VDV 749 is a 1957 Bristol LS6G, which was new to Western National. Withdrawn in May 1970, she has passed through a variety of owners and remains in preservation today.

TMS (Teesside Motor Services) KHU 316P is a Bristol LH that was new in January 1976 to the Bristol Omnibus Company. She had a short life here, being withdrawn in 1982 and passing through a couple of dealers, as well as Peter England Shirts, before ending up on Teesside. This 1991 view is in Stockton-on-Tees.

Back to Norwich in September 2006 for the Eastern Counties Omnibus Company 75th anniversary celebrations and a pair of preserved Lodekka buses passes through the city centre. At the rear is OVF 229, a Bristol LD5G that was new to Eastern Counties in 1954, while leading her is 557 BNG, an FL6B that was new at the end of 1962 as LFL57.

A Saturday morning in 1980 and Eastern Counties Bristol VR191 (TEX 401R) and Lodekka FLF444 (GVF 444D) stand side-by-side in the Old Cattle Market bus station in Ipswich. FLF444 had been new in 1966, and put in a sterling twenty years for this operator, ending her days in 1986 as a waiting room and foreman's office at Ipswich during the bus station rebuilding at Ipswich.

Bristol VR BAU 178T was new to East Midlands in November 1978, and passed to United Counties in March 1993, where she stayed for five years before being sold on in 1998 to Clynnog & Trefor for further service, before being withdrawn and scrapped in 2004. In this 1996 view she arrives in the bus station in Bedford in full Stagecoach 'stripes' livery.

Eastern Counties Bristol VRs VR191 (TEX 401R) and VR332 (NAG 587G) shiver in the cold alongside Bristol LH919 (TCL 139R) at Ipswich in December 1981. VR332 came to Eastern Counties in June 1973 as part of the Lodekka/VRT exchange between the National Bus Company and the Scottish Bus Group, having been new to Western SMT in November 1969.

The neat and eye-pleasing rear-end styling of the ECW-bodied Bristol VR can be seen in this view of Eastern Counties VR241 (JAH 241V) and VR204 (XNG 204S) at Ipswich in the early 1980s.

Bristol VR DWU 294T was working for Hedingham when photographed in Clacton-on-Sea in the summer of 2001. New to the West Yorkshire Road Car Company in November 1978, she came to Hedingham & District in 1991 via Keighley & District and Norths (dealer). She still survives today as a Play Bus in Banbury.

A pair of ECW-bodied Leyland Olympians that were new to London Transport in 1986 passes through Trafalgar Square in 1993, as C815 BYY heads D136 FYM, both heading away from central London on route 53.

Nelson Independent Bus Services of Wickford in Essex, trading as NIBS, were operating Bristol RE TUO 259J when she was photographed arriving in Basildon in 1990. She was new to Western National in 1971 and passed in 1983 to Southern National.

New in August 1976, Eastern Counties VR185 (PEX 385R) is seen here at Claydon in 1980 on a short local service from Ipswich. She became part of the Cambus fleet in 1984, then part of the Viscount fleet in 1989, before returning to Cambus in 1991. She was subsequently scrapped in 1994.

Wearing the GRT-style livery is Eastern Counties VR309 (PRC 855X), seen posing for the camera on the edge of Hollesley in Suffolk in 1999. She was new to Trent in October 1981, this being the last month that Bristol VRs were delivered. She was sold to Eastern Counties ten years later in 1991, and subsequently passed in 2002 to Jordan of Coltishall for scrap.

The full length of the Bristol RELL can be seen in this 1980 view of Eastern Counties RL513 (EPW 513K) at Ipswich. New in March 1972, she was one of the last surviving REs with Eastern Counties, not being sold on until March 1987, to Excelsior of Wellington. She was sold on to Delta of Stockton-on-Tees at the end of 1988, and scrapped in July 1995.

United Automobile Services 814 (APT 814W) was a Bristol VRT/SL3 that was new in December 1980 and was subsequently scrapped by United without being sold on for further service, date unknown. She is seen here in Ripon in the spring of 1991 before departing for Harrogate on route 56.

Bristol VR LUA 716V was new in 1980 to West Yorkshire, passing ten years later to Yorkshire Rider. Moving to Eastern National in December 1994, she was photographed in that operator's bright livery arriving in Colchester in 1996. She passed to First Eastern Counties in 2000 as a replacement at Ipswich for accident victim TAH 273W.

Bristol RELL6G CRU 137L carried ECW bodywork B45D, and was new to Hants & Dorset in 1972, passing to Wilts & Dorset eleven years later in 1983, and was subsequently scrapped sometime in 1990. In happier times with her original owner, she is seen here in 1981 at Swanage.

New in March 1969 to Eastern National, CPU 979G is a Bristol VR with the earlier flat-screen body built by Eastern Coach Works. In June 1986 she became a driver training vehicle within the Eastern National fleet, before passing briefly in to preservation in 1991. By 1993 she was part of the Northern Bus fleet at North Anston and is seen here at Dinnington the following year. She survived in this fleet until 1997, when she passed back in to preservation.

To illustrate the rear view of the earlier flat-screened Bristol VRs, here we see CPU 979G working for Northern Bus in 1994. She survives today in preservation.

Showing off her all-over advertising livery for Suffolk's two local independent radio stations to good effect is Eastern Counties VR204 (XNG 204S), collecting passengers at Wickham Market in 1983. New in March 1978, she was scrapped by the company just over twenty years later, towards the end of 1998.

One of many liveries carried by Eastern Counties VR287 (VEX 287X), she came to Ipswich wearing this dual-purpose-style livery and fitted with coach-type seating, but was used on local bus services. In this 1984 view she is in the care of the Woodbridge out-station, on a Saturday afternoon working of route 244, posing for the camera in Bredfield Road, Woodbridge.

A Saturday evening late in 1981 and Eastern Counties RL668 (PPW 668F), a Bristol RE that was delivered new in May 1968, collects passengers at Ipswich for the early evening journey to Sudbury on route 205. She was scrapped by the company in February 1983, during an era when vehicles were rarely sold on for further service.

The small Suffolk village of Dallinghoo is the location for this view of First Eastern Counties Bristol VR CJH 144V, working the rural 72 service from Ipswich to Woodbridge in the year 2000. This VR was new to Alder Valley in 1980, and passed through Alder Valley North and The Bee Line before ending up with Eastern Counties in 1996.

Badgerline's GHY 138K arrives in Wells in 1991 having worked across country from Weston-super-Mare on route 126. New to the Bristol Omnibus Company in August 1972, and subsequently Badgerline in 1986 when BOC was split. Passing to Northern Bus of North Anston in 1992, she was scrapped three years later in 1995.

Preserved Eastern Counties Bristol RE RL681 (RAH 681F), seen at Alton on 16 July 2016 as part of the popular annual weekend event. 681 was new to Eastern Counties in July 1968, and passed to Cambus on the formation of that company in September 1984. She has since worked for a variety of operators, including Buckinghamshire Road Car and Busways Travel Services (Blue Bus Services), before entering preservation in the late nineties.

Eastern National's KOO 793V is a Bristol VR that was delivered new in April 1980 and became part of their Citybus fleet for use on London's tendered bus network. She is seen here in 1990 passing through Edmonton Green working route 359 in 1990, the year in which she became part of the Thamesway fleet before being sold on to Badgerline the following year. In 1998 she joined the Abus of Brislington fleet before moving to Chepstow Classic Buses in 2006, where she was acquired for spares and subsequently scrapped.

London Transport's BL4 (KJD 404P) was new in March 1976 and by 1994, following the gradual break up and privatisation, had ended up in the Centrewest fleet, still operating in London. In this 1994 view she is seen in Oxford Street being used by Centrewest as a driver training vehicle.

New in November 1965, Eastern National's 2849 (NTW 942C) is a Bristol FLF6G that remained with the company until February 1981 when she passed in to preservation. Owned by the Eastern National preservation group she is still active today and was photographed here back in 2012 in Brentwood on the running day celebrating route 251.

August bank holiday weekend and Eastern Counties VR290 (VEX 290X) stands at Felixstowe while in the care of the Woodbridge out-station. New in October 1981, she remained with Eastern Counties until February 2001, when she was withdrawn after being driven under a low bridge in Ipswich. The strength of the ECW body was apparent after this incident, in which the roof, windows and pillars all remained intact, although she was squashed slightly!

The summer of 1982 and Eastern Counties VR398 (ENG 398K) has just arrived at Shotley from Ipswich on route 202. New in March 1972, she remained with the company before being scrapped without seeing further service elsewhere.

New in March 1981, Eastern Counties VR270 (RAH 270W) is seen at Ipswich on her first day in service. Allocated officially to the small depot at Saxmundham, vehicles between here and Ipswich were often swapped around. She passed to Jordan of Coltishall (dealer) for scrap in 2002.

New to Great Yarmouth Borough Council (later Great Yarmouth Transport) in February 1979, Bristol VR CVF 30T is seen passing through Great Yarmouth in 1997. She passed to Eastern Counties in 1996 upon the sale of Great Yarmouth Transport, and remained in her blue livery until withdrawal in 1999 due to axle damage. She passed to Jordan of Coltishall for scrap.

Red & White Bristol VR SKG 896S arrives in Newport on 19 May 1992. New to Western Welsh in 1977, she was withdrawn by Red & White and cannibalised in 1994, before passing in 1996 to Avon Fire Brigade for accident training. She ended her days later in 1996 with the Bristol Omnibus Company where she was broken for spares.

Bristol RE TWX 198L was new to West Yorkshire in December 1972. Passing to North Devon in 1984, she moved two years later to Delta of Stockton-on-Tees, where she was re-registered in 1992 as IIL 1839. She was still carrying her original registration when photographed here in Stockton-on-Tees in May 1991. She was scrapped by the company in 1994.

New to Eastern Counties in January 1975 as VR150, Bristol VR GNG 716N is seen here in 1993 passing through Slough. Passing to Cambus in 1984 when Eastern Counties was split, she then worked for a variety of operators, including, here, The Bee Line, and Taylor of Morley before being withdrawn in 1999 by her then owner Abbott of Leeming.

Eastern Counties RL728 (YPW 728J) is a Bristol RELL6G with ECW53F bodywork that was delivered new to the company in January 1970 and was scrapped without being sold on some thirteen years later in February 1983. In this 1982 view she was captured by the camera in the small Suffolk village of Earl Soham on a circular service that took in some lovely countryside.

New in December 1968 to Eastern Scottish, Bristol VR LFS 303F was part of the Lodekka/VR exchange between the National Bus Company and the Scottish Bus Group in 1973, which was when she moved south to Eastern Counties, where she remained until January 1986, when she passed to Jordan of Coltishall (dealer). Left to slowly deteriorate for some sixteen years, she was rescued by Julian Patterson and splendidly restored. She remains in preservation today and this view was in Norwich in September 2006.

Delivered new in November 1963, Bristol MW AAO 34B was originally registered 427 LAO and was held in storage until April 1964, when she entered service with Cumberland Motor Services having been converted for driver-only operation. Withdrawn in September 1980, she survives in preservation today. She is seen here at Keswick in May 1979. (Photo: Peter Horrex Collection)

Passing through Enfield in North London in 1991 is Bristol VR XHK 225X, which was new to Eastern National some ten years earlier in August 1981. Eastern National's London tendered operations were rebranded into the Thamesway name and it is this fleet name she is carrying here, though still in Eastern National colours. Withdrawn by Thamesway in 1992 she passed to Western National and remained with this operator through First Group ownership before being withdrawn and scrapped in 2004.

South Wales Transport Bristol VR ECY 988V was new to the company in July 1980, and remained with this operator until being scrapped in 1998, though she did spend a year (summer 1995 to summer 1996) working for Brewers. She is pictured here in Neath on 21 May 1992.

A damp day back in 1979 as Eastern Counties VR377 (UAH 377G) pauses at Stonham Aspal working local route 240 in to Stowmarket. New in June 1969, this is a Bristol VRTSL6G with ECW H39/31F bodywork. The exact date of her withdrawal by the company is not known, but she was scrapped sometime in the early 1980s without being sold on.

A sad sight in one of the Yorkshire scrapyards in 1994, as an unidentified Bristol RE stands alongside Bristol VR CBV 3S. Numbered 2003, this VR was new to Ribble in August 1977, and she passed to PMT before being scrapped later by that operator in 1994.

The differing rear ends of the ECW-bodied Bristol VR and Leyland Olympian can be seen in this view at First Eastern Counties Ipswich depot in 2000. On the left is Bristol VR PRC 855X, which had been new to Trent Motor Traction in August 1981, and came to Eastern Counties ten years later, surviving with this operator until she was scrapped in 2002. XHK 236X, on the other hand, is a Leyland Olympian that was also new in 1981, though to Eastern National.

Eastern Counties LH919 (TCL 139R) stands in a snow covered Old Cattle Market bus station in Ipswich in December 1981. Note the cut away from near-side corner, something common on Eastern Counties REs and LHs to prevent damage when negotiating some of the tight, narrow country lanes served at the time.

Southern Vectis MDL 955 is a Bristol LD6G Lodekka that was new in June 1956. She was sold by the company in 1978 and she passed via Norths (dealer) into preservation, before being sold back to Southern Vectis in February 1993 for use on the service to Needles. She is seen here in Yarmouth on the Isle of Wight in 1993. By 2001 she had been withdrawn and was sold on to Rexquote of Bishops Lydeard where she remained until 2005 when she was sold to Helle Iversen in Denmark, and is listed as still current today.

Eastern National 3092 (STW 36W) is a Bristol VR that was new to the company in February 1981, remaining with the company as part of First Essex, before being scrapped in 2003. In this 2001 view she arrives in the bus station in Colchester.

ECW-bodied Leyland Olympian C418 HJN was new to Eastern National in 1985 and was still working for the company under First Group ownership when photographed in Chelmsford some twenty-three years later in the spring of 2008. She survives in preservation today.

Eastern Counties RL507 (CNG 507K) stands in the summer sunshine at Claydon in 1980, having worked the short journey from Ipswich on route 218. New to the company in September 1971, she was scrapped just thirteen years later in 1984.

A side view in the snow at Stradbroke in 1982 of Eastern Counties VR204 (XNG 204S) wearing her all-over advertising livery for Suffolk's two local radio stations.

Bristol FLF6G Lodekka GLJ 748D is seen here arriving at Showbus in 1999. This bus was new to Hants & Dorset in June 1966, and survived with the company until August 1980, when she passed to Good News Travels of Hull. She later worked as a driver trainer for Millers of Chichester and then Bargoed Transport Training, before entering preservation in 1989.

The neat ECW rear-end styling of both the Bristol VR and RE can be seen in this 1981 view of Eastern Counties TEX 408R and PPW 667F at Ipswich. VR198 was new in May 1977, and survived in to the First era, being scrapped twenty years later in 1997, whereas RL667, which had been new in May 1968, was scrapped in 1984.

New to the East Kent Road Car Company in May 1980, Bristol VR XJJ 658V is seen here in Canterbury in 1994. Withdrawn and sold on at the end of 2000, she passed through a couple of dealers before ending up in 2001 with Chepstow Classic Buses, where she was placed in storage before being brought in to use in 2016.

ECU 201E is a Bristol RESL that was new to South Shields Corporation in May 1967. Ten years later in 1977 she was working for Bickers of Coddenham in Suffolk, and ten years after that in 1987 she was acquired by Busways Travel. She entered preservation in January 1998 and still survives today. She is seen here at Showbus in 1992.

Hedingham L104 (LFS 292F) is a Bristol VR that was new to Eastern Scottish in December 1968, and came to Eastern National in 1973 as part of the previously mentioned VR/Lodekka exchange between the Scottish Bus Group and the National Bus Company. Pictured here in Southend in 1982, she had been acquired by Hedingham the previous year, and survived with the company until 1989, when she was sold on to Northern Bus of North Anston. She went for scrap in May 1990. (Photo: Peter Horrex Collection)

Eastern Counties RLE869 (WPW 869H) is a Bristol RELL6G with ECW DP50F bodywork that was new in April 1970. In this 1983 view she is seen in the small Suffolk village of Brundish, working through to Woodbridge on route 273. She still survives today in preservation.

Eastern Counties RL735 (AAH 735J) is believed to hold the record for the longest running all-over advertising livery, even having a repaint in to this livery. She is seen here in Norwich in November 1977 advertising the facility of sending your parcels by bus. New in January 1971, she passed to Cambus on the formation of that company in September 1984, before going for scrap in 1986. (Photo: Peter Horrex Collection)

Preserved Southern Vectis HDL 25E on the occasion of the Alton running day on 16 July 2016. New in 1967, she was withdrawn and sold by the company in 1982.

URP 344H is a standard Bristol RELL6G with ECW B53F bodywork that was new to United Counties in December 1969. In 1986 she passed to Luton & District before being used as a mobile cafe. She is seen here parked near Harlington in 1994.

Busways 1811 (YWC 18L) is a Bristol RELL that was new to Colchester Borough Council in May 1973. Scrapped in May 1998, she is seen here passing through South Shields in 1991.

Eastern Counties LM630 (FPW 630C), a Bristol MW with ECW B45F bodywork that was new in 1965, stands alongside LHS932 (WNG 101H) at Ipswich in 1979. The Bristol LH was originally registered XXE 131H and delivered new to Luton Corporation in November 1969, but was not used in service. She came to Eastern Counties in 1970 where she was re-registered before entering service and given fleet number LHS595. She was renumbered to LHS932 in 1977 and was scrapped in 1980.

Eastern Counties RL668 (PPW 668F) makes her way through the leafy lanes of Suffolk in 1981, heading away from Newbourne to her destination of Waldringfield on route 241. New in 1968, she was scrapped fifteen years later in 1983.

Preserved Eastern National Bristol MW 7017 HK was new in 1958, and is seen here on 28 April 2013 in Walthamstow. Withdrawn in October 1970, she was acquired by Davies of Graftham, before entering preservation.

United Automobile Services 1661 (MGR 661P) is a 1975 Bristol LH that was subsequently scrapped by the company twenty years later in 1995. In this 1991 view she stands in Ripon before working to York on route 144.

The summer of 1991 and Badgerlines LHT 170L departs Wells for Taunton on route 163. This Bristol RE was new to Bristol Omnibus in June 1973, becoming part of the Badgerline fleet in 1986. In 1994 she was sold to Anslow of Garndiffaith, where she remained for three years before being scrapped in 1997.

Eastern Counties RL707 (VAH 707H), a Bristol RELL6G that was new in 1969, is seen here in Woodbridge in 1985, having been loaned to Ipswich from Bury St Edmunds depot for a few days. She remained in the fleet until the end of the year when she was sold to the Oulton Broad Yacht Club of Lowestoft. She was scrapped a few months later in March 1986.

New to Eastern Counties in March 1974 as VR132, Bristol VR RAH 132M is pictured here in Slough in 1993 working for The Bee Line. She moved from Eastern Counties to Cambus in 1994, and then on to Luton and District in 1991 and on to The Bee Line in 1993. Working for Skyes of Appleton Roebuck from 1994 until 1998, she ended her days with Stephenson of Easingwold where she was subsequently scrapped.

New in March 1981, Eastern Counties VR267 (RAH 267W) pauses in Aylsham in Norfolk, working route X58 to Sheringham in 1997. She parted company with First Eastern Counties in 2002 when she moved to the West Country to work for First Western National. She was broken for spares in 2005 and subsequently scrapped.

SHN 80L is a Bristol RELH6G with ECW DP49F bodywork that was new to United Automobile Services in July 1973. She remained with this operator until March 1988 when she entered the preservation scene. Having a variety of subsequent owners, she still survives today, and is pictured here back in 1999 at the Showbus rally at Duxford.

New to London Transport in September 1976 with fleet number BL49, this Bristol LH was originally registered as OJD 49R. She remained in use in London until 1997, though her latter years were as a driver training vehicle. Into preservation from 1997, she was re-registered in 2000 to ULO 524R and subsequently to WYL 137 in 2007. She still survives in preservation today and is seen in this view in 2010 at the Potters Bar bus garage open day.

The Suffolk village of Grundisburgh is the location for this view of Eastern Counties VR287 (VEX 287X) in 1989, wearing the livery introduced under GRT ownership. New in October 1981, she remained with Eastern Counties in to First Group ownership until 2002.

XPT 801V is a Bristol VR that was new to United Automobile Services in June 1980, and she is seen here at Ripon in May 1991 alongside Bristol LH AHN 606M that was new in 1974, and served the company for twenty years before being scrapped in 1994.

First Eastern Counties VR275 (TAH 275W) stands at Shotley in 2000 having reached her destination from Ipswich on route 97. She was new to Eastern Counties in May 1981, and remained with the company under First Group ownership before being scrapped in early 2001.

In June 1977, Bristol LH OFB 965R was new to the Bristol Omnibus Company. Working later for Peter England Shirts and Prince Henry's Grammar School in Otley, she moved to Cambus in 1992 where she remained for eight years, when she moved to Carters of Colchester in 2000. Broken up for spares, she is seen here at Carters' premises in Capel St Mary in 2001, before being scrapped in 2002.

New to Thames Valley in June 1972, Bristol RE DRX 631K passed to Eastern Counties in 1981 and was given fleet number RL687. In 1985 she was photographed at Ipswich collecting passengers for Diss on route 852 and she remained with the company until withdrawal in 1987. Working for Carters of Colchester for one year until 1988, she was sold on to Rallybeam (Blue Bus Services) of Debach in Suffolk. She entered preservation in 1998.

Another livery carried by Eastern Counties VR287 (VEX 287X) was the so-called 'Venetian blind' livery, as seen in this 1986 view at Felixstowe.

The full length of the Bristol RE can be seen to good effect in this view of Eastern Counties RL506 (BVF 822J) at East Bergholt in 1980. New in July 1971, she passed to Cambus in September 1984, before moving on to Delta of Stockton-on-Tees in 1987. She was scrapped in June 1991.

An earlier photo in this book shows Bristol RE OWC 722M in the yellow livery of South Shields Busways. She is currently preserved in this blue livery, also used by Busways, and is seen here at the Alton running day in July 2016.

Eastern Counties VR390 (BNG 452J) collects passengers in Woodbridge in 1985. The 244 service running between Ipswich and Melton on an hourly frequency was a busy route, taking in various housing developments in Kesgrave, Martlesham and Woodbridge. VR390 was new in June 1971 and scrapped by the company in the 1980s.

Cumberland Bristol VR CBV 2S, seen here in Penrith in May 1991, still survives today in Cyprus. New in June 1977, she has had many owners along the way, including South Coast Buses, Mercury FM, Phoenix of Witham and Mulley of Ixworth. She was exported to Cyprus in 2008.

New to Eastern Counties in October 1974 as RLE743, Bristol RELH GCL 345N moved on to Cambus ten years later in September 1984. In March 1989 she was sold to Hylton Castle Coaches, trading as Catch-a-Bus, and was photographed in South Shields in 1991. She had a brief spell in 1993 with Aintree Coachlines before going for scrap later that year.

New in July 1972 to the Bristol Omnibus Company, Bristol RELH6L GHY 134K is seen here at Sheffield on 12 September 1992 working for Northern Bus, who acquired her from Badgerline in 1992. She was scrapped three years later in 1995.

New to Eastern National in July 1981, Bristol VR XHK 218X passed to Thamesway in the summer of 1990, becoming part of the First Essex fleet in 1996 before being scrapped in 2003. Back in 1991 she is seen here passing through Enfield Town working London Regional Transport service 307.

New to Hants & Dorset Motor Services in March 1978, Bristol VR VPR 484S passed to Wilts & Dorset in 1983. By the time this photo was taken in 1997, she was part of the Damory Coaches fleet and is seen here on the outskirts of Blandford Forum.

Eastern Counties Bristol RE RL516 (EPW 516K) was new in April 1972, passing to Cambus in 1984 where she remained for five years. She saw further service with Viscount, Johnson Coaches of Hanslope, Buckinghamshire Road Car and Busways Travel (Blue Bus Services), before finally ending her service career

in 1998 when she passed into preservation. She is now preserved back in her home territory of Norfolk, and these photos show the neat, spacious interior of the ECW bodywork carried by the Bristol RELL, as well as the stylish look from the outside. (Photos: Neil Chilvers)

Another view of Eastern Counties VR270 (RAH 270W), this time at the picturesque location in the village of Kirton, in Suffolk, working a service from Ipswich to Felixstowe in 1995. New in March 1981, she spent most of her working life at Ipswich, but ended her days in Norwich on the Park and Ride services from 2001 until withdrawal the following year.

New in November 1977 to Western National, this Bristol VR VDV 137S has worked as both an open top and closed top bus, with the roof being removed or fitted as required. In 2002 she was photographed in Bath.

Acquired by Eastern Counties from Trent in 1991, and subsequently scrapped in 2002, Bristol VR PRC 855X was one of the best VRs that I have ever driven. In this view taken at Ipswich depot in 2000, she receives a wash and brush up before taking a well-earned rest, her work for the day done.

New in 1974 to National Travel South East, this Bristol RELH came to Eastern Counties in 1978, and became part of the Ambassador Travel fleet in 1984 when Eastern Counties was divided up before deregulation. She is seen here at Ipswich in 1984 carrying fleet number RE848 and wearing Eastern Counties Eastline livery for use between Felixstowe, Ipswich, Cambridge and Peterborough.

Bristol VR APT 813W was new to United Automobile, passing to Tees and District in 1990 and Hedingham and District in 1996. She poses for the camera here in 1996 in Sudbury on a local service to Great Cornard.

Eastern Counties Bristol VR OCK 998K was new to Ribble back in May 1972, and she was over thirteen years old when acquired by Eastern Counties as part of a batch from Ribble late in 1985. Seen here passing through Shotley in the summer of 1987, she remained with her new owners until 1990 when she was scrapped.

New to City of Oxford Motor Services in 1982, Leyland Olympian BBW 218Y was working for Hedingham Omnibuses when photographed at Mistley in 2000.

Eastern Counties VR138 (SNG 438M) passes through Lower Holbrook in Suffolk on 18 May 1993. New in August 1974, she put in a sterling twenty-three years' service for this operator before being scrapped in 1997.

At Ipswich in 1984 stand Eastern Counties withdrawn Bristol RE RL737 (AAH 737J), which had been new in 1970. On her right is Bristol Lodekka 97 TVX, which had been new to Eastern National in December 1960, and passed to Eastern Counties in 1978, where she found further use as a driver training bus. After withdrawal by Eastern Counties she saw further use for Drivesafe (Scotswood) and Youth for Christ (Driffield) before being scrapped by Integrated Transport Group of North Anston after being stripped for spares in 2000.

London Country Bus Services BN61 (TPJ 61S) was a Bristol LH that was new in November 1977. She was sold on to Hurtwood House College of Holmbury St Mary and by October 1990 she was with Blue Saloon of Guildford. In 1996 she entered the preservation scene, and was photographed here at South Mimms on 5 July 2008 on the occasion of one of the Potters Bar bus garage open days.

New to National Welsh in September 1980 was Bristol VR GTX 747W. She became part of the Red & White fleet in 1991, and was photographed the following year arriving in Newport on 19 May 1992. She was scrapped in February 1998.

Diverted from an original order for United Automobile Services, Bristol VR SNJ 592R was delivered instead to Southdown Motor Services in June 1977, passing to Brighton and Hove in January 1986. Sold on in 1995, she spent a year with City of Oxford Motor Services at Wycombe Bus, where she was withdrawn in 1996. Passing through Munson (dealer) of Hadleigh in Suffolk, in 2008 she moved across the water to Amsterdam in Holland.

New in January 1980 to Alder Valley, Bristol VR GGM 107W passed to The Bee Line in 1992 before coming to Eastern Counties in 1997. Wearing a livery introduced under GRT ownership, she poses for the camera beside the River Stour at Shotley in 2000, before returning to Ipswich on route 97. She was scrapped in February 2001.

Collecting passengers for Sudbury at Ipswich in 1981 is Eastern Counties RL501 (APW 501J). New in 1971, she was scrapped by the company in 1986.

SWN 156 is a Bristol LD6G that was new to United Welsh in January 1959. She became part of the South Wales Transport fleet in 1971 and was subsequently scrapped on a date unknown. In this view she is pictured at Neath. (Photo: Peter Horrex Collection)

New to Crosville in 1973, Bristol RE YFM 284L became part of the Crosville Wales fleet in 1986 before being sold on to Catch-a-bus in 1988. This 1991 view shows her passing through South Shields on a local circular service.

Eastern Counties VR127 (RAH 127M), which was new in March 1974, is seen here at Mistley in 1986 having arrived from Ipswich on route 123. She was withdrawn and scrapped in March 1989 after being destroyed in an arson attack while parked overnight in Sudbury.

Eastern Counties VR255 (PCL 255W) carried this all-over advertising livery for Interlink parcels back in 1985. She spent a short time at Ipswich depot and is pictured here in the hands of a Woodbridge out-station driver at Stratford St Mary on a Sunday working of route 93, returning to Ipswich from Colchester. She was withdrawn in 2001 and broken up for scrap the following year.

Eastern Counties VR405 (KPW 405L) was new in March 1973 and provided twenty years' service for this operator before being scrapped following an accident in 1993. She is pictured here in 1986 passing through Kesgrave on a Saturday working on route 83 from Melton to Ipswich.

New to Eastern Counties in 1975 as VR152, Bristol VR JNG 50N was converted to an open top bus in 1985. Withdrawn in 1997 she passed to Jordan of Coltishall (dealer) and had passed in to preservation by 2006, and remains as such today. In this 1995 view she is seen climbing Convalescent Hill in Felixstowe.

LBD 922V is a Bristol VR that was new to United Counties in 1979, being sold on at a relatively young age in 1986 to Milton Keynes Citybus, before moving later the same year to Eastern National. In 1991 she moved to the other side of the country to work for Badgerline, and she is seen here working for that operator in Bath in that year. She was exported in 1998 to South America.

New to Southern Vectis in July 1979, Bristol VR YDL 671T remained in the fleet until 1995 when she was sold to Newnham Coaches of Hook. Passing through Mike Nash (dealer) in 2004, this bus moved to Norfolk to be used as a donor for the restoration of Julian Patterson's LFS 303F, after which she was scrapped.

New in March 1981 to United Counties, VVV 954W is seen here leaving Cambridge for Huntingdon in 1996. The following year she was sold on to Premier Buses of Huntingdon, before moving north a few months later to Lochview of Greenock. After changing owners a few more times she was finally scrapped.

Standing in the Old Cattle Market bus station in Ipswich in 1980 is Eastern Counties Bristol LH YAH 909J. Given fleet number LH909, she was new to the company in October 1971, and was scrapped ten years later, shortly after this photograph was taken.

Eastern Counties Bristol MW LS835 (APW 835B), was new in 1964. In 1979, a year before her withdrawal, she is seen in the Old Cattle Market bus station in Ipswich.

In November 1954 Eastern Counties took delivery of Bristol Lodekka OVF 229, an LD5G that remained with the company until withdrawal in 1971. In that year she passed in to preservation with the Eastern Transport Collection and she still survives today. She is seen here in Norwich in 2006.

Eastern Counties LFS50, 50 CNG, was a Bristol Lodekka FS5G that was new in June 1963. After earning her keep as a service bus, she was renumbered X68 and used as a driver training vehicle. Withdrawn by Eastern Counties in 1988, the registration number was transferred to a general managers car and she was re-registered LAH 577A. She was exported sometime around 1998.

XHK 236X is a 1981 Leyland Olympian with ECW H45/32F bodywork that was new to Eastern National. Passing through Thamesway, she was working for Eastern Counties by the late nineties, and was photographed here at Ipswich in 2000.

Originally numbered 5523 in the Bristol Omnibus fleet, PEU 518R is a Bristol VRT/SL3 that was new in August 1978, becoming part of the Badgerline fleet when that company was formed in 1986. Under First Group ownership, she moved to Western National in 1998 where she worked out her days before being scrapped in 2003. In this 1991 view, she is seen in Bath closely followed by JNU 136N.

Another view of Eastern Counties RLE869 (WPW 869H), this time at Levington in 1980 working the short 250 service between this village and Ipswich.

Standing at Felixstowe in 1986 before working the return journey back to Ipswich is Eastern Counties VR191 (TEX 401R), a Bristol VRT/SL3 that was new in 1977, and withdrawn by the company twenty years later in 1997. By 1998 she had been exported to Holland and still survives today.

336 EDV is a Bristol SUL4A with ECW C33F bodywork that was new to Western National in December 1960. She is seen here in September 1992 arriving at the annual Showbus rally at Woburn.

Another view of Eastern Counties VR368 (TNG 368G), this time collecting passengers in Needham Market in Suffolk in 1979 bound for Stowmarket on route 204.

London Buses Leyland Olympian C58 CHM carries ECW bodywork H42/26D and was new in April 1986. She was captured by the camera in 2001 passing through Croydon working for Arriva London on route 264.

New to Alder Valley in July 1980 was Bristol VR CJH 143V, seen here at East Bergholt high school in Suffolk on 1 March 2006 working for Hedingham. After working for both Alder Valley North and The Bee Line she came to Hedingham in January 1995, and was exported to Starline Tours in California a few months after this photo was taken.

New to Eastern Counties as LS789, Bristol MW5G 5789 AH remained in service with the company until August 1976. In November 1976 she was purchased by Kirkley High School in Lowestoft, where she remained until June 1978, when she entered preservation with the Eastern Transport Collection. This 2006 view was taken in Norwich.

Withdrawal of Eastern Counties Bristol REs based at Ipswich began in the summer of 1984, and this photo shows RL680 (RAH 680F) in July of that year with some windows removed, and no doubt other useful parts will have been removed as well. New in June 1968, she spent most, if not all of her working life in East Suffolk.

A further view of Eastern Counties RL680 (RAH 680F) in happier times some four years before withdrawal. She is seen here in 1980 at Felixstowe having worked across from Ipswich on route 253.

Another withdrawal at Ipswich in July 1984 was Bristol RE RL667 (PPW 667F). Her working days over, like RL680 she went for scrap. New in May 1968, she carried ECW B53F bodywork.

In February 1981 Eastern National took delivery of STW 30W, a Bristol VR with ECW H39/31F bodywork. She passed to Thamesway in 1990, then on to Green of Kirkintilloch and Cambus before being acquired by Hedingham in December 1996. She was still with Hedingham when photographed at Colchester in January 2006. She was sold in to preservation in 2010.

STT 409R is a Bristol LH with ECW B43F bodywork that was new to Western National in June 1977. Passing to Devon General in 1983, she was sold on three years later to Trimdon Motor Services and then Teeside Motor Services in 1989. She was scrapped in 1995. In this 1991 view she was photographed at Stockton-on-Tees.

A further photo here of Bristol VR287 (VEX 287X) returning home to Ipswich in January 2007, having been acquired for preservation by Andy Cook from First Western National. Sadly, due to a change in circumstances Andy had to let her go two years later and she was exported to Italy in 2008.

ECW-bodied Leyland Olympian D185 FYM, given fleet number L185, was purchased new by London Buses in December 1986, surviving in London until 2005, when she passed via Ensign (dealer) to Truronion of Truro, subsequently becoming part of the First Devon & Cornwall fleet in 2008, before being scrapped later the same year. She is seen here passing through Waterloo, working for Arriva in 2001.

Part of a batch of VRs delivered new to Eastern Counties in the summer of 1976, OPW 179P passed to Cambus in September 1984. She moved to Viscount in 1989 before coming back to Cambus a couple of years later. She was scrapped in 1996, some six months after this photo was taken in Cambridge.

Eastern Counties Bristol LS MAH 744 was new to the company back in July 1952, was converted to driver-only operation in 1955, and remained with the company until withdrawal in 1972. Now part of the collection at the Ipswich Transport Museum, she is pictured here in Shotley in 2006.

New in July 1986, Leyland Olympian C108 CHM carries ECW H42/26D bodywork. She is seen here in 1993 heading away from the Elephant and Castle, bound for Greenwich on route 188.

New to Hants & Dorset in October 1969 Bristol RE RLJ 341H is pictured here working for Wilts & Dorset. After withdrawal by Wilts & Dorset in 1986 she worked for the Poole Harbour Commission for three years before entering preservation in 1989. She still survives today. (Photo: Peter Horrex Collection)

Eastern Counties VR300 (VEX 300X) was new in August 1981, passing to the newly formed Cambus in September 1984, and was subsequently scrapped in 1999. This photo was taken in Cambridge. (Photo: Peter Horrex Collection)

The final picture shows Eastern Counties VDV 752 outside the ECW factory in Lowestoft. New to Western National in November 1957, she came to Eastern Counties with sister vehicle VDV 753 in 1979. For the period from 1987 to 1999, both passed to Roberts of Croydon for preservation but were loaned to Squirrell of Hitcham in Suffolk. In 1999 the pair were acquired by Rexquote (Quantock Motor Services) of Bishops Lydeard. Sister VDV 753 was sold in to preservation in 2014, while VDV 752 passed to His Church (charity) of Market Rasen in 2016. (Photo: Peter Horrex Collection)